Reichstag Burning

poems by

Jonas Kyle-Sidell

Finishing Line Press
Georgetown, Kentucky

Reichstag Burning

Publisher: Leah Maines

Editor: Christen Kincaid

Cover Art: Rachel Herrick

Author Photo: Adeline Sutter

Cover Design: Elizabeth Maines McCleavy

Printed in the USA on acid-free paper.
Order online: www.finishinglinepress.com
also available on amazon.com

Author inquiries and mail orders:
Finishing Line Press
P. O. Box 1626
Georgetown, Kentucky 40324
U. S. A.

Table of Contents

We are Prisoners of Love

For my mom, for her championing of my work

"Yes. I was running to win. I thought we could win. But, in my heart of hearts, I knew how difficult this challenge would be."

—Bernie Sanders

Author's Statement

This book was written as two things were happening in my life: a move from the city to the county to live with my girlfriend and her kid, and the political awakening and nervous breakdown the country has encountered. It has indeed been a political awakening for me, and like a lot of people, I attribute this to Bernie Sanders.

A large part of the liberation that comes from writing and art for me has always been a freedom from the fads of technology and new world orders. Part of the way out poetry provides me is a way back. It provided me with a way back to myself and, at the time, a way out of the world of antidepressants and antipsychotics. A way back to girls and my heart and love and my hometown of Los Angeles and the bright California sunshine. A way to New York City, to friendship, to my gut and something like righteous manhood. A way to the cover and soulfulness of the Deep South. A way to sex and solitude and redemption—eventually, Baltimore, teaching, music, politics, sawdust on summer air. . . Writing is everything for me. It is work, heartbreak, and neurosis; and eventually, you break through—for that few seconds, your body filling with the euphoria and catharsis one feels during exercise, in the first part of the second half of a run, when you are fully present and your spirit is freed and the reset button has been hit. The landscape reveals itself to you, and there is nowhere to go but forward.

I think to the extent that the spirit of art remains primitive, many artists are not surprised by the current implosion of pop culture and the retreat from globalization. It's also no surprise this would manifest in the protection of privileges these forces threaten: whiteness and maleness. But the current way wasn't working either; we need something more than Neoliberalism to account for private prisons, poverty, global warming, corporate/Wall Street greed, healthcare, education, and the institutionalized racism and sexism therein. Media is now a full-blown drug and truth is on trial. To this extent, a reversion to simpler days is a natural and healthy response—one I believe artists are intrinsically aware of—but it can never come at the expense of truth and tolerance, as is happening with Donald Trump and the Republican Party. If it does, it is simply dangerous.

So now is the time, I believe, for artists and journalists and teachers to serve their final purpose. If we have plied our trades correctly, in pursuit of emotional integrity (democracy), we should be absolutely terrified right now, and extraordinarily ready.

-Jonas

Prologue: Reichstag Burning Essay

In 1933, a month after Hitler gained power through a free election, the German Reichstag (Parliament) building burned down. To this day, no one knows exactly who did it. The Nazis blamed it on the Communists and one person who was affiliated with the Communist party who had been seen around the building at the time was convicted and prosecuted.

But regardless, the Nazis were able to create such a hysteria, that the President (German power structure is different—Hitler was Chancellor at the time) granted Hitler the right to suspend their Constitution, and civil liberties therein, in order to round up the enemy: the communists, and absolve the country of this threat.

This meant basic human rights—or what we consider so—were no longer. The government could come and search your home without a warrant. You could be thrown in jail for no reason. And that's what happened. And the opposition was rounded up so there could be no dissent as further laws were enacted to give Hitler absolute power. By the end, Hitler could literally create a law and pass it in the same day without going through anyone.

And what happened next is history: World War 2, the Holocaust, Germany's attempt to become the "master race" and dominate the world. . .

The burning of the Reichstag and what happened after is a classic move from the playbook of Tyranny. It is step one in becoming a dictator. It is highly likely, and many people believe, the Nazis themselves set it on fire. But just like "Fake News"—at that point, it didn't matter. It was a post-truth world, and people were willing to look the other way in the interest of their own safety.

So! I want you to imagine something like that happens here. It has already been spoken about and written about and many people's worst fear, in lieu of Trump, is that there will be some kind of alleged or staged terrorist attack here, and everything can change very quickly. You are essentially writing stories from the future, from a future that hopefully doesn't happen. Have fun! Let your imagination imagine the unimaginable. What would you do? What are the possibilities of what could happen? Here's another key: I want you to use two sources to inform your stories, to make it grounded in history and/or reputable ideas. You can use information about dictatorships in history and around the world to inform your ideas of what might happen; there are also many things that have recently been written that are exploring/fearing this idea. You will give these sources to me in the form of an Annotated Bibliography on the last official day of class. Your story itself will not be due until finals week, on the day we are scheduled to meet. I may pick your brain for one last handwritten thing in class on the day of the final, but it will not be anything you have to prepare for or worry about—you will just be responsible for handing in your stories.

Your stories should be told from the perspective of someone alive in the future after this happens. That's the only requirement. Also, at least 800 words. Be creative!

We'll talk about what an Annotated Bibliography is.

Poems for the Political Revolution

In this life (and there is only one), you make choices, you take your stand and you awaken from the youthful spell of "immortality" and its eternal present. You walk away from the nether land of adolescence. You name the things beyond your work that will give your life its context, meaning. . . and the clock starts. You walk, now, not just at your partner's side, but alongside your own *mortal* self. You fight to hold on to your newfound blessings while confronting your nihilism, your destructive desire to leave it all in ruins.

—Bruce Springsteen, *Born to Run (The Memoir)*

A Sunny Day

It's remembering
why you came here, the feeling

        in the 3rd quarter of a run. A sunny
day   and a   good friend,

          12 years
deep. And she will not understand you

          right when
you need her to. She will not

            understand you. But she will
try, and so

             will you. And you will try
to stretch the day,   the two of you,

             into something
that doesn't seem

                 so

             finite. As if

         childhoods

       never

     ended.

The Sum of All Physical Things

Sexless
writing

is the worst, so I need—

        you

darling

      to tie
me up plain

'n simple. Tilt

your ass

to that

      moonlight, watch
me get

      —at that. Then I'll come back
and leave again, but you and I know

I ain't
goin
nowhere. I'll be here

'til the last sun
fries itself
across the windshield
of some new day, and you can fry

eggs on it. You could
fry
an egg on it. I'm so afraid

of being cast out
                         into the world again
without you. It's a constant
sunset
                   in my mind—contrasting
the sum of all physical things here, rote
edge 'n pleasure.

A World of Truth

There it is.
The core
of what tore them apart.
Their cultural differences.
Him feeling taken for granted,
and her guarding her independence.
(In a stunning cliché, he feels too dependent,
and she feels taken for granted.) The subtle insults, not
knowing each other's friends, the parts of them
not
of this—   (their)   world
staying that way.
The cliff of hurt. Before the edge: the isolation.
At the edge: the abuse. After: the blackness. The block.

I take a walk, and think about
these two characters. I think about
all that space
in their conjoined world
they are not allowed. The abuse of that space
by the two of them being there—a world of truth
slamming at the shutters, them taking it
all out
on each other.

       That world of truth is this: time
       is not on their side, so as it
       passes, it steals a little bit of
       the present, 'til there is nothing left

           except
           everything they were trying to keep out. The remnants
           of their fears, which, without the love
           serve
           no purpose. It's just aloneness now, but at least there's room
           for a decent conversation—

And there it is. I walk, and think about
these characters, how quickly
the hot center
can explode, how maybe   time's cruel joke is only
that the work gets clearer, which is really not anything at all.

Breadth of Ocean, Depth of Sky—

and uncharted, like everything else

try your best
to bleed the sea
through your nose
and know the truth
ain't always true

in this fucking life. Gum drops

we are captains
of infinity, ragamuffin
beaches—no noise
to drown us out, but we scream
and nothing comes out.

and compulsions, most questions

Hapless

are answers to the void. I was responding

sex, helpless
love, there's a small window of opportunity
here. Like composing a poem
on several
different
mediums, when the words and lines
come out the same. Pencil and notepad
will suffice. Pencil and notepad

to an emptiness inside me. I still am.

will always suffice. The word they tell you
never to say, the word
they assign
meter to, is rhythm, and it's the only thing
that matters. It's inscrutable, like the air—

Shuckster

You're like come on the duvet cover, darling, dirty
and sweet; and here are my fists clenched

to a sack of roses. No one should believe us. Every flare
has flown, shot from behind

those stories of love
by correspondents   who

think they've pinpointed   its failure, and are calling
for our rescue

after theirs. Well—
think again

shucksters,   I want not to be rescued
from the mother of her landslide, and I want not to be rescued

from this sincere powerlessness. This is it: the dirty life and times
of getting exactly what you hoped for, which is to say

something
I can't

shake. The sun slides down, the birds chirp, a hammering
somewhere

in the grassroots of time (I write at the kitchen table, now! instead of my
dingy room)   and consciousness, that sleek green

bent on continuing—a cat asleep
next to me. Let's move into the light, darling

with *almost*
as much

darkness
to give.

I Miss Charles St.

Poetry at least can sizzle between the mundane.
Take anxiety
and make it shallower. Take light

       I'm wondering how I will carry the things
       that have always carried me. Am I doing right

on a wall,
lying flat on your back
on a bench, and make you think

       by my family? Am I doing service
       to the pursuit

of Germany, some flat—some life,
somewhere.
We get by, knowing

       of love and poetry
       that has

only what we think we know, and what
we intend to—
—take something

       unwillingly devoted itself to me, taken
       me in, given me a night, mornings, breath, eyes,

and make it political,
but not. Take a cop car

       a cloak, an identity, a long
       black coat (I was always

and make it see red. Take a nap. Take
too much tequila, screaming child, weed

like clouds, summer

     much too giddy), what, oh what
     will I do now

sheets. You can do anything
with poetry. Take a walk
to the watering hole, the Wawa,

     that I have another place to live?

and call yourself a mystic. Take one day, one life,
and make it not feel like a waste of time, take one night—

When Everything Moves Too Fast

You tell the pain:
you can live without me.

We've come this far,
but you go on without me.

I'll catch up
in a little while.

Because there's something
adrift in me, like a cast line, that I want

to stop.

I want to zero in on something. The blue sky
of angels, the message

of might—if we're willing to admit
evil exists,   we must acknowledge

its journey
in our own. It's all we've got

for the kids.

Feel You, Feel Me

It surely had to do
with not overcompensating,

learning to live honestly,
learning to write honestly.

It certainly had to do
with a hunger for truth.

Call me an Empath, call you
a Narcissistic,
this is our
toxic relationship—

but the lines are skewed
and the mirrors

choppy, you've got to angle
it

right, and that just has to do with
your word against mine, and the time

divided by imagination,
multiplied.

What We Were Talking About

Because we were young once
and we're not old
yet. Because the body
of time and love
is not just a carcass;

it lives—

because regret comes in the form
of dispossession, a lingered patch
of hollow air
along the trail; something we only did

in hindsight—

because each time we've just learned
how to survive, a new threat
is born, like trying to remember
what we were talking about, and no one

taught us
how to globalize.   We just shifted—

Power in Power

There's no power in power, no
beauty in geist—the spirit concedes

> *We become the enemy*

to the animal. And as you climb the ranks,
the animal takes over,

> *to keep from becoming the victim—*

unless you are careful. The spirit becomes
threatened, and begins to prey. Love cannot

> *More power in power, more*
> *beauty in geist*

be preyed upon, so the scent of fear
becomes familiar, this slight ingratiation, subtle breach

> clack clack clack clack *the animals*

into cozy denial, for a moment.

> *alone at sunset.*

Grown Ups

Our only job
        is to stay young. Who aspires
                to adulthood, besides

kids? You ratify it. You
        roll with it—   try
                to stop it,   'fore

it's
        too
                late, 'fore

that last
        glimmer
                of irresponsibility   turns

into the latest piece
        of technology. But wait! kids like
                technology. So maybe

we just cusp the evening
        with all that we've got. Draw dots in the air
                where the digits should be, chase Pokémon

like un-admitted
        sex fantasies. Say it: *what a long hot summer*
                of injustice

in this country. I will not lose you to the fire.

Like Falling Rock

The sun scores the evening
like a falling rock. And everybody knows
the best moment
for a poem
is right before the first word—so this one
is already tainted. Art must first
resist specialization. *You have my time*, it says.

Where the Contradictions Meet

Chinatown bus and whiskey in a knapsack. Don't I have a say
in any of this?

This world full of kids and music.

Bernie Sanders in the dark. This poem is dissembling itself

    right out of town—

        preoccupied, still, by the dirt
        and spoils
        of a sunroof, I saw; it's entire history

Not enough time. Not enough time
to disappear into that heavenly aloneness, etc.:
harvesting stillness

where the contradictions meet…

    windows   windows   windows!

full of intellect.

I got a Facebook reminder, today,
of a photo
from a friend, from two years ago—

of a post-it
he put on my box, that said: *Your poems still suck. Nice hair.*

Post-truth—

We can lie to ourselves
here. The threads

snap, and
spin-off

our faces
and bodies, here—   land

at our feet:

loose,

and dusty

you. It would make more sense
if I were talking about

someone in particular, but this is a
post-truth you, this is no one

in particular. This is a media-tapped
you, eponymous

anonymous, *symbolic*
you. We are living in dangerous times,

noise and light
beats out metal in the dark, and the prisons

are left standing. Someone is the culmination
of his or her experiences, someone packages them

along the way. Along the way, someone brands them—
he or she

is the culmination of the packages of his or her experiences…
but they have never been put that neatly

in a box. Nor are they
            here, lying

                    at your feet, gleaming
                        self, now, shed

                                of it, ready for the next question.

Words are the Relevance of Our Time

This expresso moment, spinning
top,
   and nobody knows
what anybody else (really)
goes through? As if this panic

were mine (but isn't that the definition
of panic)—

    this post-truth, era,
like a post-it. *If words mean nothing,*
then actions mean nothing. I began wary

of the written page, believing movements
trivialized my pursuits. (That they were just words.)
But I'm starting to think
I was wrong. What good is this
set of particles
if we just

blow it apart at the end of the day?

There is more than just circumstantial evidence
for this.

An idea
sprung from the mind,
garnered through experience,
constantly   relocated   in the heart.

What I find myself
constantly wanting to say
about everything
at the end of the day,   is yes, this means something.

A Horn like Trust, We Blowin'

It takes a still stolen moment
to sink one. Even if it floats right back
up
you felt its weight—and outside, the day

drifts. Another one, and she is asleep—
we made love—
even through
the broken glass—and the kid, who is not

here yet, but who is
already here, not mine, but mine, is cosmic.
Who knows
how this shit works.

You just keep trying
to sink one. That's all I was doing
anyways; and I'd rather do it
here. Outside, a long way from

Hipsterville, or Middle America (closer to
the latter), some kids shoot hoops. They took
the other basket
down, because they would come late at night,

and shine headlights, and drink—so
the court
is now resigned
to half. Further outside, the country

splinters. I want not to think about
my own lost innocence, or the fact
that I need to make more money. I'm a gentle man, thinkin' 'bout

                                    family
                                        what I have to do next
                                            and poetry. Let me be here,

jaded and clean, a long way from nowhere…

Easy Truth, Not that that is Love—

Because I am always lonely
without you. And that's not
a birthday wish,
Christmas gift, errand run
or chore

done. I'll simply take
the notion of being with you
against that
of not, anytime
anywhere.

Because there's a rhythm
when I hear
family. Something always
moving—not a comfort
in the darkness—but a comfortable

darkness. Incontrovertible, even if one
allows, as one
should, for our separate
traumas. I have tried
to disprove it; come up with

islands
made of sand. The already
given. Easy truth, not that that is love—
I want a world
written to the cadence

of great works of art
with enough room
between the lines
to scroll our own screed—if there is not
enough room

we will make it… This is just another poem

I have written
pledging myself
to something beyond
islands made of sand. To something beyond

the ruination of sex, and the rejection
of poetry. Something beyond
white supremacy, chauvinism, American
consumerism. Something, now,
fascist-fighting, vibrant-democracy-

upholding. There are no easy truths.
They just make me lonely. And that's not
a birthday wish,
Christmas gift, errand run
or chore

done. I'll simply take
the notion of being with you
against that
of not, anytime
anywhere.

Interlude: Liberal Media

I grew up in a liberal household where there wasn't much distance between who you were and who you were supposed to be. My mom is a social activist, and politically minded to an extent that I will always only be able to aspire to. I grew up watching her slay the dinner table in thorough and vigorous, and sometimes heated discussions. I admired, was in awe in fact, of her conviction on what was happening and what should be happening, and secondly, her ability to express it solely based on that conviction. She didn't have an echo in the wings or a hand on her shoulder, it was just her, paving the path for forward thinking, thinning their arguments through details and misconceptions and "the other day I was talking to. . ."

I wasn't around many conservative people, honestly. All my friends were mutts and I myself was half culturally Jewish and half whatever else. It was Los Angeles in the 80s and 90s and though I was unaware of anything but basketball, soccer, how low I could get away with sagging my pants and if I could pull off headphones around my neck all day, crack had tore through modern civilization and the cops were benefiting from it. Hispanic immigrants were holding up the economy but couldn't get a valid driver's license. West L.A. gleamed and Beverly Hills was actually made of glass, though it was a good place to skateboard. And in the middle were all the shades of normal life, compounded by a certain diversity—work, leisure, lust, exercise, kin, and the palm trees, oh yeah, there, twinkling in a reed-thin dusk. The sunset lighting a fire behind Santa Monica.

But I suppose I was aware of something off in the distance, like a pitch of noise that would, if transcribed, amount to a dot, resembling what people deemed the Republican Party. I had heard the discussions, felt the opposition, even if it wasn't in the room. What I was aware of was the existence of a certain obtuseness, an insensitivity, a—well—a lack of awareness! I was aware of what I was learning in the history books, and I could imagine it in some of the guys on the basketball court. I could imagine it in the motherfuckers who bullied me for having big hair. And I already pitied these guys.

But whatever it was, once in the political realm, I gave it some release. I figured there were separate political discourses, legitimately, that spawned from different warehouses of thought. In tenth grade, in 1996, after we moved to Georgia, I proposed a bill to make gay marriage legal—but that was only because I was so shocked that it already *wasn't* legal. Now the dot was getting bigger. Still, even in my incomprehension, my guffaw, I attributed it to some higher thinking, a difference in choice. Surely this grown up thing called politics—the running of our daily lives in the most efficient and fair way possible, the outlying structure given by us to keep this beautiful and natural world rolling down here on earth—could not just be blasted from the hip. The arguments at the dinner table were remarkable for their reverence and attentiveness, and respect. Where was the other half of the argument? The policy discussions and waves of historical repetition being analyzed and revolutionary sentiments amidst outright disgust being expressed were never trivial, sensibly there had to be other reasonable opponents, contrary policy-makers. Surely there were people of other viewpoints doing this same thing somewhere, strategizing by a cool night, candles, a vase filled with flowers.

But I was wrong. And there is one reason for it, a reason so ingrained in the human dilemma that it somehow becomes exempt: bigotry. What we were fighting for was exactly that: reverence and attentiveness, and respect. The arguments were secondary to the fact that we were actually arguing. Which way the candle flickered didn't matter so much that we had one lit—

racism is no more intentional than being born into one's skin is, but that doesn't make it any less real. Racism can be innocent, in fact, but that doesn't make it any less sinister. If race itself is not real, but a fiction of power, the cause of racism not only is irrelevant, it's void of truth. It doesn't fucking matter if you intend to be racist or not, action is the only plausible deniability. The Republican Party, of modern American history, has always had its superego greased in the same oils as slavery, and with Donald Trump, we watch it rise to the surface, unadulterated and bare, without even the cloak of an agenda. Let me be clear, that in my opinion, any person who votes for Donald Trump in this country, of any race or intent, has the blood on their hands of a slave owner. We now know what the Republican party really is.

Enough

I would no more
       put other people down, than I would put
          myself down

Trump called
       Iowans stupid
          at their own rally—

an advent
       to superiority/
          inferiority

I wanna wake up
       to a morning
          that is enough

The sun requires
       no faith!
          as it shines   over

all our things,
       a glass ceiling

I'm still trying
       to gain access
          to your womanhood

It's written in the books; it's written in
       the absence
          of material things

And we feel it on long walks
       and we appease
          our incessant

ignorance
       of things

I can't understand
        how one would ever respect
                someone

for calling them stupid—
        the prospect
                of doing the same to someone else

But it must never be enough.

The Shape I'm in

As I make my weld from never-hipster
to almost-family man, and I've used up
plenty of my liver enzymes by now—

perhaps it skips a generation, my dad
and stepdad
always felt the weight of a certain line

my brother and I like to toy with. Danger
is escaped, never obvious. The soul crushes
to test for heat. I'm still a writer-who-has-

to-act-like-he's-playing-in-order-to-work,
no office, nuanced reception just-enough-to-
stave-off-completely-unsentimentally-acting-

like-I'm-leaving-even-though-I-never-would-
cause-I-can't, here's another fucking poem
to light

your world. The political revolution
is one child's dread and wonderment. I'm going
for a run. Tell the kids

next semester
to trust themselves only as far as they can fling 'em,
that nobody-really-has-any-idea-what-they're-doing.

(in the Age of Post-truth)

In this sense, Trump's election was enabled by the neoliberal policies of the Clintons and Obama that overlooked the plight of our most vulnerable citizens. The progressive populism of Bernie Sanders nearly toppled the establishment of the Democratic party but Clinton and Obama came to the rescue to preserve the status quo. And I do believe Sanders would have beat Trump to avert this neofascist outcome!

–Cornel West

A New Paranoia

The ascent can never outweigh the de—
the nights
blowing through a 3rd story window;
a figure there
still—

and then I find myself
open to being open
again, realizing the pain
was more like a bad habit   (I think)—

time expands. California still drives itself
into the sea. But here, any notion   of the ocean
cuts itself   in streetlight
and 1 dollar crabs. A new paranoia

talks election politics
through the soul of a poet, and remembers how
children   are
locked behind their eyes. There's nothin' to do

but watch *jadedly*
without yet
any sure knowledge of death. But it will
come,
it will—

and we will climb
the mountain, bloodied and freed, if the ends
are not separate from the means, if the ends
are not separate from the means.

Truth to Power

The birds rule these suburbs
and the path to sustainability

is in a cockeyed plant
and art

        that still smells like 25th St. . .

Baltimore, I can hear the sound

of an unguided moment
opening, something tearing

through, past the rubble
of neurosis, a zipper

in the air—
        if something is stolen:

-----

when the needle hits the groove,
the light bows

in the backyard, then we've got
work to do. And *fuck. party. unity.* these old

Democrats, complaining of
insurgency—you reap what you sow.

        And the Republican party

-----

has always been a disease: a conflation

of church and state
in Washington, to cover up

moral infidelity
at home.

The distance between

-----

your public persona
and private need

is the level in which you will self-destruct.

These Long Hours

You can't overcompensate. The day
will find its way
in. The night

will

too. These long hours
of waiting, for your unpledged

desires
to declare an early victory—
        There is a problem, here, and I can't quite

put my finger on it. But it might have something to do
with one side being represented
                         by a truly vapid celebrity, a waste

of our time, and the other, now, by a political dynasty
remembered fondly
for boomtime. 2008 we were so fucked

we had the guts to believe. Now we're much better off
so we choose not to fuck with it. This was a safe bet,

this was a let's-not-rock-the-boat thing. And it seems to me
that everybody who is not pandering to Obama, that anybody who knows

he fucked up the learning curve a little bit, that he missed a lot of chances
to talk to us—that we expected more—knows Hilary is not that, either.

We will get more unpledged desire
and early victories—

Poems for the Political Revolution

I have tried
to negotiate myself—
      what I felt was true,
      what I see in my head,

into this physical world. Ideas
are just ideas. Feelings

are just feelings. They mean nothing
unless they shine a light—a true

                ra-
                dia-
                tion

of energy
onto a marked surface. Already tattered? Already

almost forgotten. I have tried
to push that into a book, to form that physical objection
of myself, fickle, feckless, shorn, insistent (what have you done

to me
girl?) it may be. The physical world
has always scared me; I do better

with the space between,

where words
have the potential
to arrive, and actions
merely hang
on that notion (get 'em, Bernie
Sanders, at that

restless podium)… I have always believed in touch, though. Always believed
that somehow

is the key—because *what*
is the alternative?

Can't Cry. Can't Scream

That muffler ain't love. That music
ain't soul. This country

be dicey. *You think it's hot here? Well...*
A sign says, along Windsor Mill Rd.

Meanwhile, carnage
employs itself

in real time. I can't remember what it's like
to talk, speak my mind. It says,

I'm barely gonna make it
this week, today. I think of a shinning morning

blowing down 25th St. I think what the last seconds
must have been like

for Philando Castile / trapped in a bathroom stall / bleeding
out on the street—narratives

intertwined,
almost taking from each other. It's too much to hide.

The injustice is total.

Neoliberalism

So the rivers flow, the sky
is still blue, rain punches

so the revolution
so the revolution

so we have Hillary Clinton
so the revolution

so the energy recedes,
the coming together—three drifters

in a park: *wasn't there supposed
to be a political rally here?*

Goddamnit Cornel West's
got it right. This neo-fascism,

this losers and winners; this
free market place, this

free trade. The truth is out, folks:
whatever this is, created corporations (including

you know who), siphoned money
from the middle class, since

the 1970s, made (in either cause
or effect) the poor feel like they *should*

be poor, and the rich
rich. A weird kind of

euphoric dementia, trickling down like
euthanasia. The problem here is:

when your faith

in our competence, Madam,

seems to require
silence

and prayer.

Make America Great Again

The dark is thick out here
in the county. We are Men of Letters,
even before—that separation
didn't separate us

from ourselves, we just started to draw it
into words. Complacency
be the enemy,
just

to keep up—Time
is no friend,
but a source. What we live for
is this:

the moment
your search for legitimacy
stops
you listen to that thing inside of you—

poems be harder to come by
these days, over-saturated by media
full of conspiracy theories. What we know is this:
you can't calibrate racism, if you can't

admit privilege, or lack
thereof. What we know is this: it
exists, and for that reason
there must not be a God. It ain't

up for discussion. Let's remove it
from the discourse. Even if it's keeping you
good (supposedly), it's keeping you
tied up. Walk this earth

knowing only your feet
bind you—that even those

can be taken, and you'll see
we all in this shit

together. What Millennials know is this: *we want
transparency. We want
in.* The lesson of the youth of every generation
is a hunger for truth, and for everyone else

to remember to afford it. I throw my
button-
down
over my face, now, in the library

of the school I teach at, lie back
on one of the chairs, so no one
can hear me think—because the feeling
in today's climate is

it doesn't matter. And that's enough
to make anyone want to
disappear. What I know is this: *you can't
go back.* Love is full-blown, if not

ready, telling its story
in the middle of nowhere—hate—on the contrary—
walks back through the front door
without even an explanation.

White Men

I always thought something would bottom-out. The dwindling
bookstores. Libraries cast-out, their tangible products
left only for the disenfranchised. All around the blooming media

creating a false composure—or lack thereof. We have over-communicated.
Awarded too many useless masters degrees. And the swing to the right,
and the swing to the left, are both trying to downsize. Re-simplify.

The victory of globalization, though, and maybe the reason
we reached through the wires
for each other

is a diversity. An un-whitewashed humanity. A De-Europeanized
earth. Bigotry was the battle of the baby boomers. Millennials
have global warming. Generation X—we're still trying to goat

Tinder. Still, in this pendulum global economy, censored poverty and
pornographic wealth—there is one faction who *reeaaalllyy* seems to be
upset: White Men.

Can't even see the good that's happening
within the mess. He must really hate himself.

Dakota Access Pipeline

This really is the future
of fucked up right here. Big money interests
versus the opposite, the primordial, and the long under-talked about
5th class citizens of this country

who were here first. This is climate change, this is poverty, this is
race, police brutality, this is—astonishingly (and this is how you know
a real nerve has been nicked)—a threat to free speech. Free speech?!
Journalism! Protest! Literature! It's what Lawrence Ferlinghetti

fought for when he published *Howl.* This is a country
literally built off the backs of the citizens it treats the worst. And
that same belligerence
has always been applied to the earth. This is such

an amalgamation. This is The Left, worried about the right things. This is, of course,
not on the presidential political map. This is what neither of them are talking about.
Jill Stein was there. Bernie was there. Hillary Clinton? Not really. Trump? Not
a chance.
This is consciousness, a moral economy. The competition
of the marketplace
doesn't win. It

conglomerates, we lose. We all will lose—but there are those with private land
who will sit back
and say, *Hey, whatever will be will be.* Laissez-faire, baby. The money
is stacked against us. A rolling storm, rolling the hills. We're not moving.

3rd Party Politics

You have to be willing
to go your own way. Find people
who make you do that.

A man walks in fall leaves…

I've never been a 3rd party person, but the debate
is much too narrow. (These people
hate each other too much.) I cast my vote
out of hope, and fear, but mostly, I must

admit
out of fear. Let it be known

that I stand
ideologically
with another country. One who chooses
not to dignify that.

The World Over

I think we've forgotten how much America has ALWAYS been an asshole.
Slavery was / is profitable.
Slavery made / makes America "great," a superpower.

I don't know who first entitled the White Man, who made them
the stewards of the world. But I believe America was somehow at its birth—
was it a blindness perpetuated by grief? What was our toil?—particularly emboldened.

We must have deemed ourselves the stewards of the world. And we must
have deemed
           ourselves
white. By some measure
of weakness, the world over, the only people who had any say

in this
were men. These were the fathers
we broke away from, grew our hair long

to piss off, dated outside our race
because we loved—the fact
of it pissing them off

only adding
to the urgency. And now somehow the stewards are back. Thee whose
rightful country
this is not. Stand with Standing Rock! Maybe Capitalism cannot withstand
the forces

of a global economy. But hasn't it always bred
the exploitation of labor, enforced by systematic dehumanization? And we got rich,
and richer
as a country, as an oligarchy. You can't have a system

founded on competition
if the market is not fair. And so the Democrats
worked to level the playing field with affirmative action

and assistance, resigned to it—Socialism, at its root! some things
never for profit—and the
        Republicans
whined about higher taxes—UNTIL, UNTIL! it wasn't about the taxes anymore, it
was about
the very jobs themselves. *Until the Republicans weren't the benefiter, anymore,*
of an uneven
        playing field;

until America "wasn't great anymore," because now they're the ones
who might need public assistance; oh   these stewards!
Now, this Caucasian cacophony, prideful, vain, hurt; found someone who still believes

what they already fear is not true, like its 1492, walking ashore: and
combined with
corporate media, and law enforcement, including the FBI… we have fascism. Now
we have fascism.

Scared White People (We're Still Here)

There's light
standing beside ourselves.

A heart-shaped
tree.

Half of what we say
means nothing, half of what we do
means nothing. Maybe the other halves

can fold

into something

hard

and true!

I guess we had a choice
      'tween doing the wrong thing
for the right reason,   and doing the right thing
     for the wrong reason—

and we fucked ourselves. White people, now, you're no longer the default
race—you've got a target on your back. Now you're going to feel what it's like

to be exploited. Liberal elite,
it's been nice knowing ya. I watch the sixties
disappear
in a magician's cloud, then reappear
right where it began. It's time
to reassure these sparkling maggots of power and cowardice, including
scared white folks
we're still here. We've beaten back

pain that took a wrong turn
before, turned it right into

progressive
song. People vote when they're inspired, and nobody likes
rich people's art, cut for rich people. Best of misguided
intentions, they couldn't swing it. And the only art the Alt-right
has
is hate. That won't work either. It's time

to scrape the knife
dull
before we mount the piece,   drain the paint
'fore we hang that thing.

The intolerable lesson
has been learned again, en masse: there's nothing worse
than scared white people.

Reichstag Burning

If one part
of the government
can seize power
by setting the other part
of the government

on fire, and then blaming
that same part
of the government
for the inferno—then you have

created, in full life, the govern-
mental equivalent
of the
psychology
that is needed, and of the, sure, hurt

that is needed, to walk around
on this earth, as an imploding
egomaniacal
masochist—what we politely
term *bigot,* but is more
accurately rendered

terrorist. A governmental
Frankenstein, unleashed
through sheer
preclusion. We've
really
done it, this time.

We are Prisoners of Love

Before German Democracy could thus be downed this week, the Hitler Cabinet had to launch last week a juggernaut of super-suppressive measures & decrees for which they needed an excuse.

–*Time* magazine, 1933

Forgiveness is Braille, or, How to Read

Our selves will inevitably disperse—
    each day
  we practice
     saying goodbye.

Kids—and one
     in particular—know
  how to do this
     effortlessly.

They have no trauma
    yet, no egos;
   no reason to hang on (which is perhaps why death
     feels so unreasonable, to them).

And one day, when we're old, if we've learned
    how time
  does not erase trauma, just turns it
    into Braille…

But for now, he only knows
   a few words.

Prisoners of Love

Even hurt
      can be mistaken for vanity.

Even love
      can be mistaken for malice.

Even music
      can be mistaken for injustice.

Even choice
      can be mistaken for freedom.

      Try it backwards:
every single one of these can be reversed.

You don't win.

I am not gaslighting you! But I have been gaslit
before:

           I have been felt crazy

for my own sexual logic—but those two words, I'm afraid,
do not go together.

I have been told, many times, that my experience
is incorrect.
           And I have been told, many times, otherwise.

You travel the roads
of truth, and you realize

the least we can do

is not be told

we're nuts. Listen, pay attention to this, it's more important now, than ever—
we have hit

a critical mass

in this country, our bodies: *get out* and/or
get over it

no longer apply.

The Set-up:

It can never be too much of a
set-up. The preparation

will bust you—
       the problem with poetry

is poems. The problem with work,
jobs. And the problem with love

is people. And right therein lies
the beauty—

       the problem with politics is
money. The problem with race

is race. And the problem with family:
bein' stoned. I love you, life. No

problems
here—

Interlude: My Own Democracy

We were children trying to figure out how to hasten the sun, bottle it, for it was always never-ending, a kind of mutiny—sprawling insurrection that was our promise, threat, caption, joy, and most of all, right. My brother and I grew up on either side of a Boulevard, called Pico, where on one side and further up it, was our dad's house. Here we had more neighborhood friends, and would play outside, usually across the street, until twilight nixed the day.

"Dinnertime!" My dad would yell from the walkway of our bottom-floor duplex apartment. And we'd run in, eat, and perhaps then it was homework time— or maybe we'd had to have it done already in order to go out and play initially—and perhaps we would go back to the others' house after dinner to play more games in the dark. I remember bedtimes at my dad's house, reading lamps on the walls of our bunk beds, feet shuffling by in the light under the doorway, late-night thoughts, first inklings of poetic dread as I fell asleep wondering how *this* could all end.

The morning would come with such an explosion of sun (or lucid grayness) that I would never remember.

Down the boulevard and across it—more and more doable by bicycle—was our mom's house. A top-floor duplex apartment with a steep driveway and massive deck outside. We had a little basketball hoop out back where once I backed up into my brother's eye and swoll it shut. My mom and stepdad had parties, gatherings, hang-outs that beat back the twilight then night outside on that surreal deck. My brother and I would fall asleep on their bed lying on our stomachs watching Double-Dare on Nickelodeon on their *bigggg* TV.

When girls hit, one time my brother and I managed to argue down our dad into letting us stay at a community center all-night event. It was like a filibuster, going all the way to the point where he came to pick us up, soaked from the indoor pool and bursting with pubescent exuberation and hormones—he caved. It was supervised, after all. We'd won, and didn't sleep a wink. I don't remember much of the teenage soirce that night, but I remember somehow arriving home in the dog-eared morning. Yeah it was love.

In tolerance and creativity, the four-set: mom, dad, stepdad, and stepmom, bounded us in physical and psychological nurture, tenets of some democracy that is the only thing I will always know forever.

As traffic increased and the middle-class was squeezed, we migrated southeast. I slipped into an immutable daze and my brother, not knowing how to fail, tried to make the best out of it. The forces gathered around us and ergo other peoples' rules and regulations, smock sensitivities, traditional verbs and nuclear family proclivities, we were from L.A., muthafucka. But that didn't last *too* long, although we relished the sound of our hometown. And we missed it; and we were allowed too. Arrogance formed out of loss is a badge of youth, and though the chip eventually gets chiseled away, its very existence is what shoots you into the next phase. But you will need someone to talk to. My parents understood all of this, and forgave us our ignorance, but neither would they shut up about it—particularly our mom. If we are put here to validate each other's torrential beings, we are also meant to challenge them. Argument is the soul of Democracy. She was not raising dictators and she was not raising slaves. And you could smoke pot and drink along the way, but just don't be too foolish!

There is a scene that always plays out in my mind. It happened a thousand times and it happened once, it happens every day and it will never happen again: there are other people over, it is either my mom's, dad's, or eventually my stepdad's-though-technically-no-longer-my-stepdad's house, at some point in our childhood, teenagehood, or young adulthood; whosever house it is, we are all there: my brother, me, our two half-sisters, their mom, even our third adopted sister; our stepdad-though-technically-no-longer-our-stepdad's new step kids are even there; everybody is talking, new significant others and semi-significant others litter the room; the people over, friends from some walk and wine of life, are trying to figure out the score. *So you were married to who? You? And these are your kids? Whose kids are these?* And we're all sitting at the table, laughing as if this is the way it has always been.

Colluding

Stay up and drink
fight the night
take hits
from your pipe
the moments
move fast (moonlight
cutting) committing
to anything
means walking
'longside
your own
mortal
self—maybe she and I

are ready to do this, and that's
the only difference   the answer
to the demons
still in my head. To walk alongside
myself; to walk alongside
her. 'Twas the immortality
throwing saucepans
at my stomach; that she could never
be anything but mine. Like how Hillary
crushed Bernie's campaign. And Russia
crushed hers. Now Donald Trump
will be president. And Bernie
coulda won. We imagine forces

of Time
swinging from sets of gymnastic
rings, giving dap
to each other

                    and we lose

our own Democracy,
        our own living thing

Only the Sane will not Survive

This is a national gaslighting.
This is a whole lot of misdirection
trying to force us to disengage—
which would not be an unhealthy

reaction. The men and women
who did just that,
looked the other way
as people and families disappeared,

were *listening*. It's a natural response
to look for places
that tell you
your experience is true, not to spend time

in the areas
you're being lied to. So we
shrug it off, and say *hell, why not?* And we
climb into bed with them—even as we're looking

the other way, 'cause we must
go on, right? It's like your partner saying to you, as
you cry, *"are
ya done?"*

Confirmation Hearings/War Crimes Trial

Take everything you've said, everything your body
   and mind
     have weathered

and build a tunnel.
   Stay low.
     These bastards

don't even have the integrity
   or imagination
     for hindsight.

There's no need to shout: these men
   and women, and those—
     are already dead. *We are those*

here in history, blanketed
      by the untold pages
        of books.

But we will not die, and we will not be
      written off—

this is poems for the political revolution
    (in the age of post-truth)
        we are prisoners of love.

What We Are Fighting For

It rained for days after Trumps inauguration. January
      21st, the day
      after, the streets
      flooded, in a women-led
      protest. Most places, too many
      even
      to march; we just stood, surrounded by
each other, never mind the bad weather, our homes bodies
our country, now claustrophobic: we are our own

          echo-chambers, nothing in our lives
          prepared us for this. Or maybe
          everything did. I feel a clarity
          and pride, that the road   I've traveled
          does not reflect
          the man, and men, and even women
             these women, and men
          are protesting against. I know I am antidotal. Those who aren't
          are probably not here. I rove
          to the outhouses, and Maxwell's *This Woman's Work*

               flutters from the stage, it's broken hymn, it's upright spine
               skittering out
               ragged
               and fine, an eternity
               of clothes on a line. On Wednesday, the sun
               cracked
like a egg, at least on my street, and this is no second chance, this is, at best,
a reckoning.

Epilogue: Jonsena 'n' Doddy

They said one small missile burned down the White House. On the morning of October 13, 2017 Americans and the world awoke to the molten ash and embers of a new reality. The visual was stunning. A collapsed roof and the remains of long pillars and studs, leaning inward and outward, where walls used to be. The damage was total. Smoke simmered into the air and then up to the blue sky before it dispersed.

It'd happened around dinnertime (the night before), and the media of course blitzed. If Prince's death was known to most, because of social media, within ten minutes, the White House in flames was pretty immediate. The fire itself was put out pretty quickly, and the world was left with the exorcised bones of the emblem of the free world.

Jonsena was in his apartment near downtown Long Beach, CA, stoned out of his mind when it happened. The palm trees danced upward to the sky, caught in the cusp of evening, as usual, when he received a text from his brother. *Turn on the news, dude,* it said. He did. MISSLE STRIKES THE WHITE HOUSE, LEAVES IT IN RUINS in red letters at the top of the screen on CBS. Jonsena thought this was probably not the best time to be stoned, and half-heartedly regretted it, before he opened and closed his hands and remembered how sore they were from working construction all day. Then he was glad he was stoned again. He walked to the window and opened it and felt the teeming air blowing in off the harbor. A woman walked by on 4th street carrying bags of groceries in both hands, a small child following lazily behind. Seagulls bent and bowed on the ocean breeze, in the shadow of the sunset, orangutan sky. Streetlights hadn't yet come on and somewhere a car radio crooned, boomed, and bopped. It was all as it should, three-thousand miles away from the fire inside the TV, Facebook, Instagram, Snapchat, and every news outlet in the world.

Doddy was in D.C., but in her bed already reading a book. She had no idea of the news. Outside her window the black sky caught barely a few stars; the streetlights warmed the brick, leaves already beginning to turn. Her black dreads fell all over her pillow and she turned to the night. She thought about the guy she'd been with last night. *Ish.* They'd had dinner and drinks at a neighborhood spot and took no time to get busy. Ach. What'drya gonna do. She'd let him come back to her place. A rare event. She closed her book, took no time falling asleep.

For many this was not a surprise, but some stone cold inevitability, like a bad dream that you know means something but you push it off—then finally you have to break up with the person. For many this was the worst case scenario, after the worst case scenario of Donald Trump being elected president, this was the worst case scenario that followed. It was not a surprise; it was a surprise. Jonsena and Doddy woke up the next morning to their cell phones ringing.

Jonsena, in his surreal state the night before, had continued partying a bit before crashing and convincing himself none of it was really true, kind of like what the whole fucking country did when Donald Trump got elected, for those who had not gone to sleep early expecting a forgone conclusion.

Jonsena came from a conservative family, kindly enough. They all had equal parts. Mother, father, uncles, aunts, the kids: Jane, Tabitha, Oreo, and Jonsena. Two girls and two boys. The mother, probably a little to her dismay, stayed home, raised the kids—worked some part time jobs teaching science labs at local community colleges. The father was a trucker, but with a decent schedule, where he was only out for four days at a time. They struggled at first, then made it to a nice spot in suburban Baltimore.

Doddy came from a liberal family that was liberal enough, with the exception of her father, who was a revolutionary. She had no rules, no real regulations; she was an epistolary. Black dreads hanging down her back like snakes—weirdness was currency, and the voice of her father kept her cutting into the hegemony, and though she did not act much, she had a dream that consisted of making him proud, and of also really doing something that had an impact—that equaled in real life the true fire she felt in her bones. She never had any money.

It wasn't the missile into the White House, though, it was what happened three surreptitious weeks later. It was the bomb dropped on Flint, Michigan. It happened in the middle of the night, and the News burst with the news of the third largest bomb to the atomic. In Trumps first hundred days, the largest next to the atomic was dropped on "militants" in Afghanistan. This—however—was second largest to that, and it was dropped on the same place that fed its children lead poisoning through the governor's approval.

So the first incident quickly faded to the second. Jonsena and Doddy were back in Baltimore. Each of their parents beckoning them the moment the news of the missile into the White House arrived. They never knew each other, until they sat down at Terps and each ordered a Natty Boh:

"They're announcing we're fucked. Civil rights done. The government can come in. That's it." Doddy said sadly, to Jonsena, as they found themselves sipping piss beer on the Thursday of the apocalypse. Neither of them had steadies or lovers. Well, a few of them lovers, but none of them steady. So there they were.

In the moment of the final fading out, nobody will really ever know it.

That's the impossible. That's the moment a plane takes flight, either fire or air. And then it *does*—it takes *air*.

Media notwithstanding, media withstanding, the drone was Donald Trump, on the TV above the bar, talkin' about war:

I KNOW THIS INTERVENTION SEEMS UNNECESSARY, BUT I PROMISE YOU IT IS. . .

he shouted into a microphone placed strategically right outside the White House with the wreckage seething in the background. . .

WHAT HAPPENED IN FLINT, THAT MUSLIM TERRORISTS WOULD WIPE OUT ONE SQUARE MILE OF ONE OF OUR BEAUTIFUL TOWNS, IS DISGRACEFUL. . .

Just as the country was still reeling from the images of the White House, an explosion rocked the Midwestern town of Flint, Michigan. Yes, this was the same town poisoned by lead water in the last couple years, through the governor's skimping of costs by not over thinking the rerouting of water from a nearby water source. Yes, this town was mostly—if not all—African American. The bomb was not atomic, but still a mile wide in its destruction. Homes, schools, and churches in pieces. Body parts in the streets. Whole bodies everywhere. The landscape scorched. These were the pictures broadcast on CNN, CBS, MSNBC, NBC, and especially FOX news. These were the pictures that punched a nation still spinning from the physical destruction of its top government building.

WE DON'T KNOW WHO DID THIS, BUT WE KNOW IT WAS SOMEONE AFFILIATED WITH THE ISLAMIC REVOLUTION. TO PROTECT OUR DEMOCRACY, WE MUST STOP IT. I AM ORDERING THE IMMEDIATE DETAINMENT OF ALL KNOWN TERRORISTS AND TERRORIST SYMPATHIZERS IN THIS COUNTRY. . .

"Yes, I see it." Jonsena replied dazed back to Doddy, while gazing up at the TV, which showed this man and his bluster peaking, reaching its inevitable form, style, and content—this prospect, this emergency, this untruth, this situation, always hidden in the dramatic inflection of his tone. Now we were where we were always gonna be since the day he got elected. It felt inevitable; it felt, almost, normal.

For a moment Jonsena forgot all about it and was caught by the sunlight coming into the bar and refracting off Doddy's clear brown-black skin and sharp jaw. Her lower lip un-pinched, slack. Her face unsurprised and ready: a cultivated anger coming to the fore.

"I'm Jonsena," he introduced himself to her.

"Doddy," she replied, caught, too, by the realization of his face. By some idea that he seemed fully inhabited in his own body.

Outside the day was like any other. Afternoon waning, shoppers in and out of stores, cars passing, love neutralizing angst, angst smiting love. People going home to their homes, their sanctuaries, their work; loved ones on their minds. Those who tell them everyday *from here on out you're not alone,* on their minds.

ACKNOWLEDGMENTS

For each of their different worried, loving, and delighted looks. Dan, for your music, Dad, your ease. Cameron, your reflection. Ruthie and Leah, your separate injections. Brandy, your challenge. Addie, for your love and defiance, the way your love has defiantly changed my life, for your love. Extended family, original and new, I absolutely cannot count! You guys are all there. This is my democracy. My friends in time, Baltimore and beyond: Noah, David, Chris, Mague, Kishan, Willie. You fill up a room. Rachel, your artwork consumes my poetry.

To the future members of the families. Little Mason, whose life I came into and who mercifully accepts me over and over. For my students, there's no such thing as teaching, all learning, you are the ground and the sky, in whatever weather.

Finally, for what we will surely go through in the next four or eight years, or longer, and what we have gone through and will go through again, and how we will rise. You can't alienate the young folks and expect peace. This is a staggering lapse into cynicism, not to mention a corporate slaughter, and it's the youngest voting generation, who voted overwhelmingly for Bernie Sanders, who we have failed the most. I'm here to tell you they will not be stopped.

And thank you Finishing Line Press, for allowing a thirty-six-year-old man to finally grow up, by publishing his book.

www.ingramcontent.com/pod-product-compliance
Lightning Source LLC
Chambersburg PA
CBHW021158090426
42740CB00008B/1139